LISTEN! LISTEN!

Can you hear that?

DRUMS!

TRUMPETS!

Something exciting is com[ing] that promises to dazzle [us]. It's the great **ANORAK** Wild beasts from lands fa[r away], clumsy clowns, intrepid unicyclists, they are all here ready to entertain, amuse and surprise us.

Let's follow them, dear friends, all the way to Anorak's Big Top for hours of rib-tickling, jaw-dropping and heart-stopping **ADVENTURES!**

Hold onto your popcorn bucket and let's go!

GOOD STUFF

Monster Mania!

Cuddly monster maniacs, listen up! We have discovered an awesome monster factory! There's Kevin with his stripy socks, who has an irrational fear of sharks; there's Darryl who likes to eat popcorn with too much butter and there's Baz who is covered in tattoos but is actually quite shy. We dare you not to want to adopt them all!
www.monsterfactory.net

Tiny but fun!

Imagination, nice drawings, notebooks and stickers – all stuff that we love. That's also some of the brilliant stuff Tiny Universe is made of. We say yay!
www.tinyuniverse.co.uk

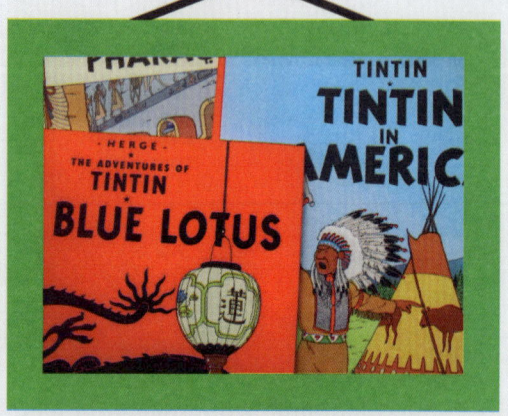

Collecting is cool.
Collecting Tintin comics is even cooler. We are 100% obsessed.

Bear on a bed!

Mum! There's a bear on my bed! It's a lovely bear though so we are quite happy resting our heads on his face. He is part of a great new home range by our friends at H&M. Instant love.

www.hm.com

Cutest of cute!

Cute and cheeky bowls, plates and even money boxes to make our dinners and savings so much more enjoyable.
www.camilaprada.com

Topsy Turvy Talk!

We have some gigantic news to share: we have invented a language! It's called Topsy Turvy Talk. It's a kid-only language, so no grown-ups allowed. Here's how to speak Topsy Turvy: you today how are? Happy back you are at school? Now it's your turn!

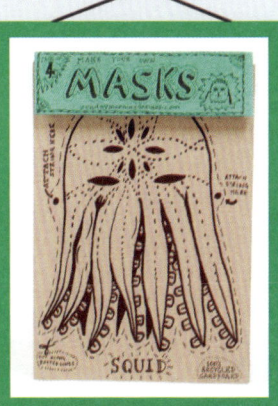

I want to be a squid!

That's lucky because we have just what you need: a squid mask beautifully drawn by one of Anorak's contributors, Dylan Martorell. You'll have to colour it in before you wear it. No ink in this squid. Get it?!
www.sundaymorningdesigns.com

DIY Tees.

These great tees are waiting for you to flex your colouring muscles. All you need to do is get some fabric paint or pens and add colour to them. And wear them with pride!
www.angelachick.com

We Save the Queen!

With this lovely costume, complete with (fake) bear skin hat, Her Majesty can rest assured that she is safe. We'll make sure of that.
www.hedgehogshop.co.uk

Colour Me Good!

Oh no! Mimi's wild birds have lost their colours. It's down to you to make them beautiful and colourful again. When you finish colouring them in, please don't forget to send your masterpieces to the lady who drew them, Mimi Leung, as she will exhibit them on her website. Turn to the back pages of this issue to start your colouring mission on Mimi's birds.
www.ilovemel.me

READ STUFF

The perfect pet shop by Vivian French (Orion Books)

My favourite bit was when the dog said "Woof! woof!" and the guinea pig said: "Tell us a story." It was very scary when the cat came to eat up a mouse. The book was lovely, thank you for the book.
- Eddie (6 years old)

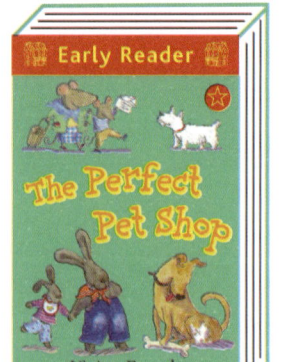

The Buttons Family by Vivian French (Walker Books)

I loved the book so much. I really liked Cherry's shoes that she chose. The pictures were very fun to look at. I also liked the very last picture in the book.
- Madelyn (5 years old)

Kentucky Thriller by Lauren St John (Orion Publishing)

I find the story is great and the writing is excellent. I love the characters and the mystery of the story. I especially like the part when Laura goes into the haunted house. I find it interesting because I have never actually been into a haunted house before. I like the writing because it is neat. I like the characters because they express their feelings a lot.
- Tuesday (9 years old)

The Secret Garden by Frances Hodgson Burnett & Inga Moore (Walker Books)

Please can I be in your next Anorak magazine because I'm reading a book called the Secret Garden? It is a very good book because there's a beautiful girl called Mary from India. Mary always had her Ayah to do everything for her, until her people got a disease and her Ayah fell ill with it and died. It's been around for a lot of years. Inga Moore, the illustrator, has done a lot of fascinating drawings. It is a great book that anyone who is nine years old and over would love to read.
- Isabella (9 years old)

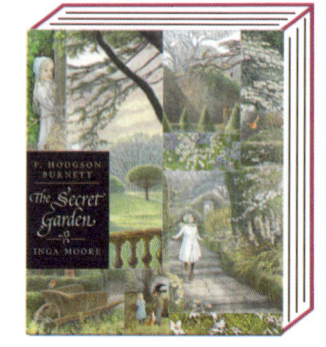

Fright Forest - Raven Boy and Elf Girl by Marcus Sedgwick and Pete Williamson (Orion Publishing)

When I opened the envelope with this book in it, I instantly recognised that it was by Marcus Sedgwick as I have read the 'Raven Mysteries', one of his series!
It all starts when Raven Boy, a nature lover who can talk to animals, falls out of his tree and squashes flat the house of Elf Girl, a magic bow wielding girl.
Then they realise it all happened because of a giant ogre who was pulling up the trees for the Goblin King, who wants to rule the kingdom. Elf Girl and Raven Boy become friends, find a rat, escape from some trolls and find a witch who knows everything in the darkest part of the forest. Turns out it was guarded by a ferocious beast... a kitten!
The book is all about never giving up and believing in yourself and others.
This book is one of Sedgwick's best and the black and white illustrations really pull you in.
I recommend you read it, otherwise a giant troll will eat you! (Just joking!)
I really recommend this book to 7-12 year olds as some of it is quite scary.
I would give it 5 stars out of 5
- James (9 years old)

The Great Piratical Rumbustification
by Margaret Mahy (Orion Books)

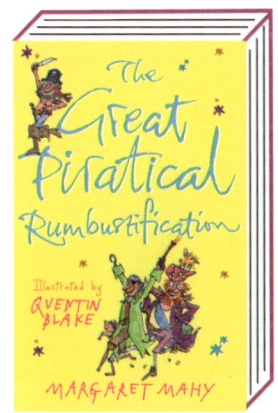

I LOVE THE STORY! It is a very funny story with a pirate babysitter. The stars spell out in the sky that there's going to be a pirate party called a rumbustification. The party happens at the house where Orpheus Clinker is babysitting, so the children get to join in. The illustrations are very detailed, attractive and funny! They suit the writing very well. I love the pictures very dearly, they are very good.
The characters are funny. Like Crabmeat, because he's got a funny wheelchair with a horn. He drives extremely fast in his wheelchair. The other characters are the pirates who come to the rumbustification and the Terrapin family, who hire the pirate babysitters. The children are funny and wild like the pirates.
Mr Terrapin starts off grumpy but when he goes to the rumbustification he becomes wild and crazy, like his children and the pirates. I think I would show it to all my cousins that can read because they will love the Quentin Blake pictures and the crazy pirate characters.
- Magnus (7 years old)

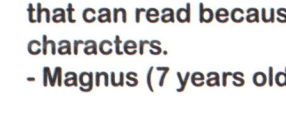

READ STUFF

Tony Robinson's Weird World of Wonders: Egyptians.
(Pan MacMillan)

I loved the book. It had Gods, Egyptian language and even explanations on how people got mummified! I loved the Gods the best because there are lots of them to choose from. I liked Ra the best. Ra is the God of the Sun.
- Jasper (7 years old)

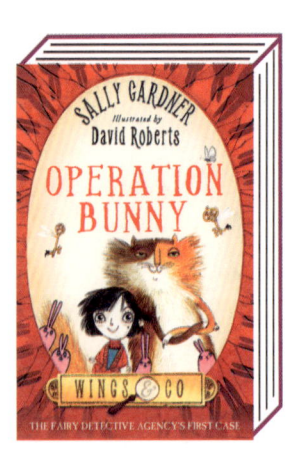

Operation Bunny - Wings & Co
by Sally Gardner (Orion Books)

Dear Anorak,
Thank you so much for the book.
I really enjoyed it because some parts were very tense and some were very funny and made me giggle. The part that made me really laugh was when a passenger on the train, speaking on a phone, got turned into a pink and purple fluffy rabbit by Harpella, the Queen of witches! Also, my favourite character is Emily Vole because she is very adventurous, brave and independent - a bit like me.
I normally don't read stories involving magic but this one I couldn't put down!
I would recommend this book to children who like adventure and powerful magic stories. My book rating is an epic 10/10!
- Eloise (9 years)

Poison Most Vial by Benedict Carey (Hachette Publishing)

I think it's a good book but the language is a bit hard to understand. I still don't really get who killed the guy! I would recommend this book to people aged 9-12, if they like murder mystery stories.
- Katinka (9 years old)

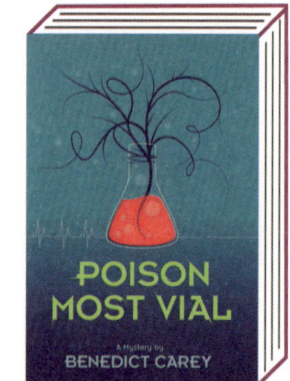

Olivia and the Movie Stars by Lyn Gardner (Nosy Crow Publishing)

Olivia is a pupil at Swan Academy, a school of the Performing Arts, where her grandmother is the head mistress.
She loves it there, she has many friends and enjoys practicing for the end of year shows. One day Olivia overhears a threatening call telling her grandmother that the school must be shut. Olivia is shocked as this is not only her school but her home!
And if this isn't enough, Olivia is also given the job of teaching two very famous, but hopeless, twins to act as they have been chosen to star in Peter Pan. Will they pull through and can Olivia save the school and the show or will it all become too much?
I thought this was a good book and I really enjoyed reading it but I would recommend it for younger readers. So for those reasons I would give it three and a half stars out of five.
- Molly (11 years old)

The Youngstars by Ursula Jones. (Inside Pocket)

It is about twins with totally different lives; a tale of love, laughter, tears and showbiz! I really enjoyed this book and I would happily read it again.
What starts off as a mysterious, slightly confusing story, turns into a thrilling page turner, which I would happily give five stars to!!! It made me cry at times but with such a mysterious and exciting story line and characters it was thoroughly enjoyable!
A FANTASTIC read! I would recommend it to ages 10+ and especially to those who are interested in showbiz. (Like me!)
- Catryn (11 years old)

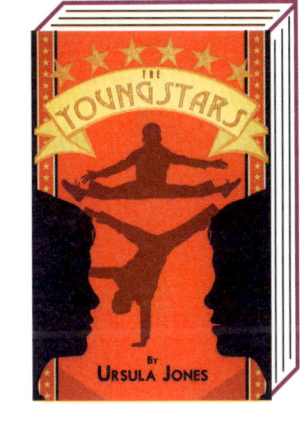

The Donut Diaries of Dermot Milligan (Random House)

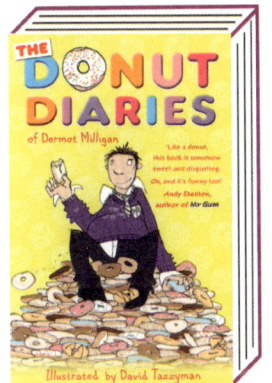

The Donut Diaries was very funny. If you like Mr Gum books and 'Diary of a Wimpy Kid', you should read this book. The book is set in three different places: 'big school' (as Dermot Milligan calls it); the park and Dermot's house. As well as being a diary about the many donuts Dermot eats each day, it is also about Dermot going to high school. It would be a great book to read over the summer holidays if you are starting 'big school' in September. It has very good illustrations by David Tazzyman, who also illustrates the Mr Gum books. I would recommend reading this book if you are nine and above. Overall, I would rate this book as 7 out of 10.
- Dexter (8 years old)

Illustration by Simon Wild.

Munkie & Horrace

Brian Munkie was in a mood. He had woken early to the sound of his best friend Horrace Harold crashing about in the garage.

He peered round the back door and saw Horrace getting out paints and brushes.

'Yippee,' cried Munkie jumping up and down.

Munkie loved painting. It was one of the few things that he, Horrace and Uncle Morris all had in common. He loved the smell of the paint, the feel of the paint and the fun he had when painting.

In fact there was only one thing Munkie didn't like about painting. And that was other people looking at his work.

HORRACE ALWAYS WANTED TO HANG MUNKIE'S PICTURES ROUND THE HOUSE.

BUT MUNKIE ALWAYS TOOK THEM DOWN.

'I LIKE PAINTING, BUT I'M NO GOOD AT IT!' MUNKIE SAID. 'PLEASE DON'T PUT MY PICTURES UP. THEY DON'T LOOK LIKE ANYTHING.'

'THEY DO TO ME,' ARGUED HORRACE. 'AND I LOVE THE COLOURS AND THE PATTERNS. PLEASE LET ME PUT ONE UP.' BUT MUNKIE REFUSED.

A FEW DAYS LATER HORRACE CAME HOME VERY EXCITED.

HE GATHERED THE FRIENDS TOGETHER AND SHOWED THEM THE PIECE OF PAPER HE WAS CLUTCHING IN HIS PAW.

'ART COMPETITION. WINNING ENTRIES TO BE EXHIBITED IN LOCAL GALLERY. FAMOUS ARTIST DAMIEN WURST TO JUDGE TOP ENTRY'.

MUNKIE SCOWLED. 'I'M NOT ENTERING AN ART COMPETITION. I'M NO GOOD AT ART!'

'YOU ARE,' MORRIS AND HORRACE CHORUSED TOGETHER.

'WHY DON'T YOU DO A PAINTING FIRST AND THEN DECIDE IF YOU WANT TO ENTER,' SUGGESTED UNCLE MORRIS.

'I THINK I MIGHT TAKE MY INSPIRATION FROM DEGAS,' SAID HORRACE THOUGHTFULLY. 'I LOVE HIS DANCERS.'

Horrace immersed himself in the graceful world of ballet.

Splashes of pinks and purples flew from his brush.

Finally his masterpiece was finished.

Uncle Morris headed down to the beach for inspiration. He had a little snack while he thought about his painting.

He was feeling inspired by Turner.

He filled his canvas with a pastiche of yellow, green and blue.

MUNKIE, HOWEVER, COULDN'T THINK OF ANYTHING TO PAINT.

HE FINALLY DECIDED TO PAINT HOW HE FELT RATHER THAN WHAT HE SAW. FURIOUSLY HE STARTED, COLOURS FLYING FROM HIS BRUSH. HE WORKED IN A FRENZY UNTIL HE WAS FINISHED.

HE STEPPED BACK FROM HIS WORK. 'RUBBISH!' HE DECLARED ANGRILY.

HE TORE THE CANVAS FROM THE EASEL, SCREWED IT IN A BALL AND THREW IT ON THE FLOOR.

THEN GRABBING HIS FAVORITE FOOTBALL, MUNKIE HEADED TO THE PARK. 'HOW STUPID TO THINK THAT AN IDIOT LIKE ME WOULD BE GOOD AT SOMETHING CREATIVE,' HE GRUMBLED TO HIMSELF.

A COUPLE OF HOURS LATER WHEN HORRACE AND MORRIS RETURNED THEY FOUND MUNKIE'S CRUMPLED PAINTING.

'OOH,' SAID HORRACE. CAREFULLY HE FLATTENED OUT THE CREASES. 'IT'S BEAUTIFUL,' HE SAID WISTFULLY.

'I KNOW,' SAID UNCLE MORRIS. 'LET'S ENTER IT INTO THE COMPETITION ON MUNKIE'S BEHALF. WE WON'T EVEN TELL HIM THAT WE'RE DOING IT.'

TWO WEEKS LATER UNCLE MORRIS AND HORRACE PLEADED WITH MUNKIE TO COME THE THE EXHIBITION TO SEE THE JUDGING OF THE BEST PAINTING.

'PLEASE COME,' BEGGED HORRACE. 'BOTH MORRIS AND I HAD OUR PAINTINGS ACCEPTED FOR THE EXHIBITION.'

'OK,' SAID MUNKIE. HE DIDN'T REALLY WANT TO GO, BUT HORRACE AND MORRIS WERE HIS BEST FRIENDS AND HE WOULD DO ANYTHING FOR THEM.

'COME ON,' CRIED HORRACE AS THEY MADE THEIR WAY TO THE GALLERY. 'IF WE DON'T HURRY WE'LL MISS DAMIEN WURST AWARDING FIRST PRIZE.'

AS THEY SAT DOWN THEY WERE JUST IN TIME TO HEAR MR WURST MAKING HIS SPEECH.

ART COMPETITION
POINT CHAV AUCKLAND

'I AM PLEASED TO ANNOUNCE THE GOLD MEDAL GOES TO . AN UNTITLED WORK BY BRIAN MUNKIE. BRIAN, PLEASE COME AND ACCEPT YOUR AWARD.'

THERE WAS A KERFUFFLE AT THE BACK OF THE ROOM.

'WHAT??' WHISPERED MUNKIE TO HIS FRIENDS. 'BUT HOW???.. I DON'T UNDERSTAND.'

'JUST GO AND ACCEPT YOUR PRIZE,' URGED HORRACE. 'I'LL EXPLAIN EVERYTHING LATER.'

'I'M NOT SO BAD AT PAINTING AFTER ALL,' THOUGHT MUNKIE AS HE ACCEPTED HIS AWARD.

THE END...

emma and nathan 2012 ©rubbishcorp

INVASION OF THE BLOBS

A long, long time ago, in a galaxy quite near ours, there lived millions of Screws. The Screws lived a very peaceful life on Screwpiter, thanks to Professor Charlie Screw, their Screwy leader. He was a karate black belt and amazingly clever, as was his cousin Professor Ben Screw.

Now, Screwpiter was a very hot planet where it never rained but that didn't matter considering that Screws never drink.

Recently on Screwpiter things had been changing: Charlie and Ben had glimpsed a big lump of blue goo sucking up one of their fellow Screws.

Words by Dexter (aged 8)
Drawings by James Clapham

They immediately ran to their rocket car to find out what this lump was and what it was up to. But, before they could catch the mysterious 'Blob', it caught them and threw them in prison!

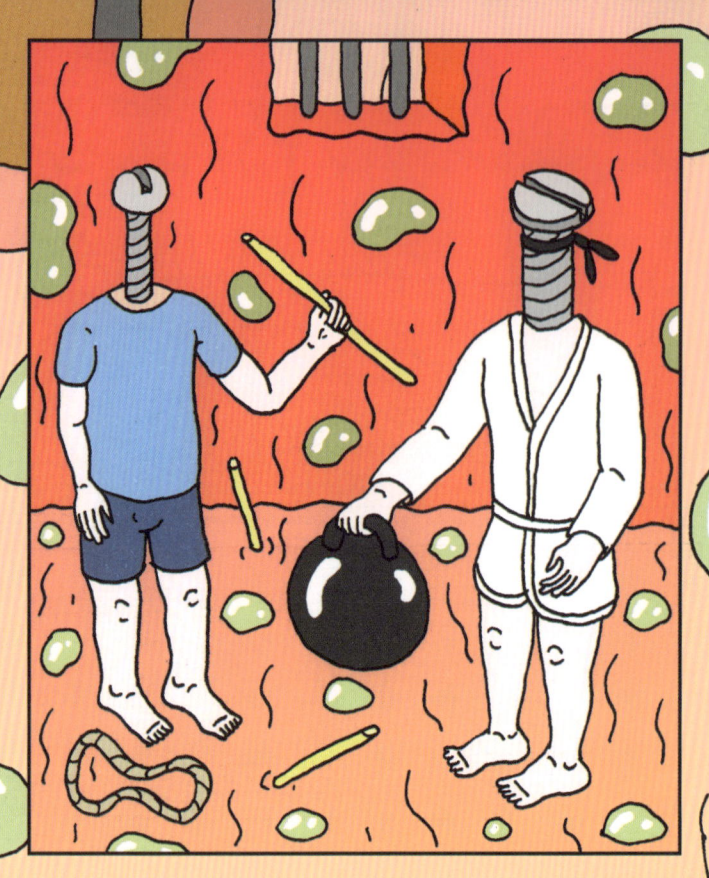

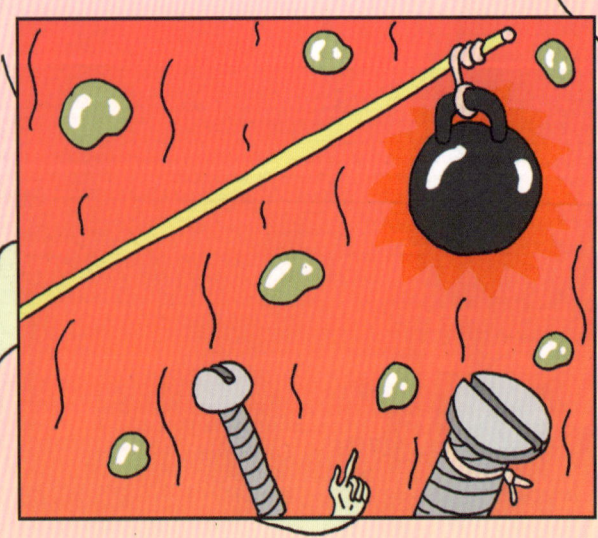

They found themselves in a dark, sticky, gummy cell filled with piles of junk and other captured Screws who told Charlie and Ben that they were in Blob-Quarters, the Blob's base. Once their fellow Screws had told them all about Blob-Quarters and the Blobs' plan to create an army of Blob-Screws in order to take control of Screwpiter,
the Professors began to think up an escape plan to get out of this wretched place...
A week later the amazing, mind-blowing, daring and dangerous plan was ready.
Charlie and Ben had discovered that the Blobs had been capturing the Screws and had been covering them in Blobbiness. This made the Screws behave like vicious, nasty Blobs.
Now, if only they could work out how to change them back...

They made a wrecking ball out of the junk in their cell.
Charlie yelled: "One, Two, Three, SMASH IT!!!!!!!!"
The Screws threw the mini wrecking ball, crushed the wall of the cell to smithereens.
They were now able to escape from the gloomy prison. Their swords were hanging in chains a few meters away from the cell door; as they ran out, they seized them and whizzed out of the building. The Blobs spotted them getting away and followed them out into the burning hot desert. The surprised Blobs grabbed their Blob-a-Paults and a Blobby fight began.

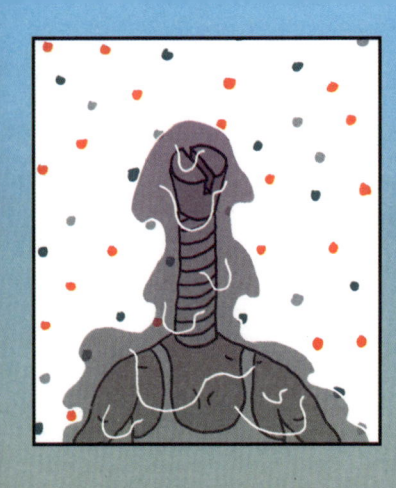

The fight went on for ages, but slowly the Blobs started to dry up and harden in the frazzling heat.
Then Charlie karate-chopped a Blob so hard that it shattered to bits and underneath the goo they saw a Screw. It was the same one they had seen being captured a week ago.
The other Blobs were also turning solid, so they did the same thing to all of them – HIIIIIEEEEYAH!!!!

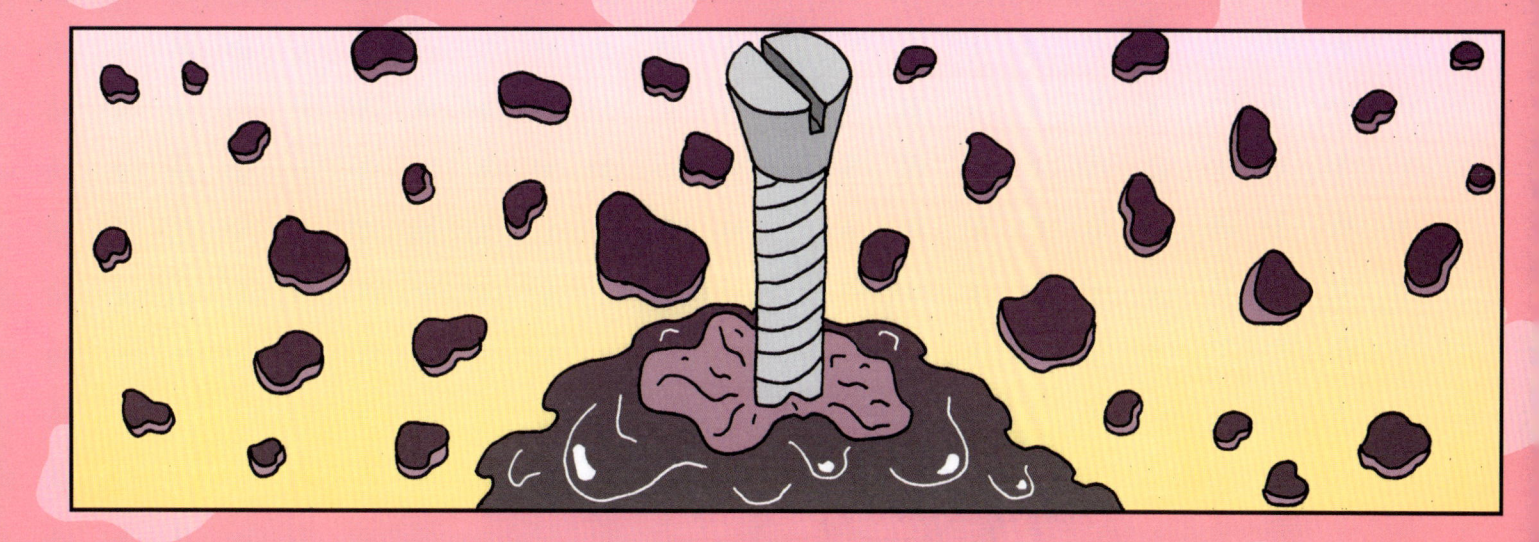

The Screws inside were free! Feeling furious and helpless, the Blobs realised they could not win and so they ran extremely fast back to the safety of their base underground.

Elated, amazed, exhausted and triumphant, the screws knew that their troubles were over.

They had a massive party to celebrate and Charlie and Ben were given amazing, golden medals as a reward.

TEDDY

Words by Cathy Olmedillas / Illustrations by Simon Peplow

Hello, I'm Teddy.
I am a travelling teddy bear.
I have been to many wonderful places in the world but my favourite is by far my bed.
That's because I like to sleep a lot.

I am very lucky as my owner, Louis, loves travelling. Everywhere he goes, I go too.
I usually travel inside his rucksack, with my head poking out so I can see the whole world.
He insists on that, which I think is rather kind of him.

The hottest place we've been to is Kenya. I got so sweaty my fur almost fell off.
The coldest place I have ever experienced was London in the winter. It was snowing everywhere and my fur froze. Snow is strange, isn't it?
It looks all cosy and fluffy but as soon as you step on it - ouch! - it freezes your paws.
My favourite place of all time is Tokyo. I was treated like a king there and got to cuddle many people.
A lot of people shouted "KAWAI" at me, which means 'cute'.

I come from a long lineage of distinguished bears; in fact you can trace my family back to Germany at the beginning of the 20th century.
Tod, my great great grandad, belonged to the Sullivan family who famously invented tea bags.
Tad, my great grandad, was definitely the coolest teddy of my family as he was instrumental in the invention of the Frisbee.
My grandad is retired now, he sits on a bed all day, but he had a fun life.
He accompanied a rock star all around the world.
I have followed in his footsteps, even though I am yet to have seen as many cities as he has.

Louis and I get on very well.
He loves cuddles and so do I, so that makes us best buddies.
He tells me great jokes, like: "How do teddies keep their houses cool in summer?
They use bear conditioning." Funny isn't it?
I wake him up every morning with a little dance and a song.
The first time I woke him up showing off my bearwalk skills, he laughed really hard. I was a bit shocked at his reaction because I thought I was doing a good job. Oh well, I guess my chances of becoming a professional dancer are rather slim with these massive paws of mine.

A HA HA!!!

Today we are off to watch a football match. I am in two minds about it.
If Louis' team scores, he gets very excited and he ends up throwing me up in the air.
I know it sounds like a lot of fun but frankly it does make you dizzy.
Let's hope we don't score too much!

TOBIAS

WORDS BY
CATHY OLMEDILLAS

ILLUSTRATED BY
EVGENIA BARINOVA

THE SUPER FLY ATHLETE.

Tobias has a dream. He dreams of being the world's best shot put athlete.
Every morning he gets up extra early.
He trains in front of the mirror,
in his bedroom, with his favourite red ball.
He rests the ball on his neck.
He puffs his cheeks (all shot put athletes do that, he has noted).
He spins, spins and spins.

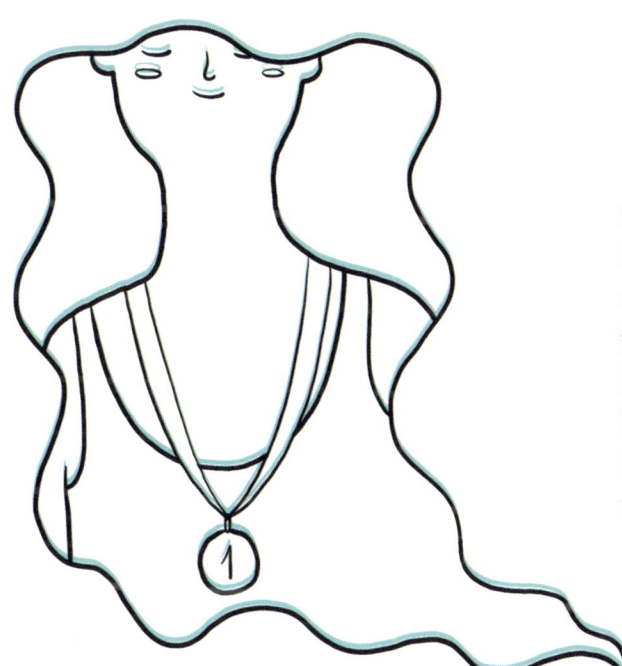

Off he goes!
He throws the ball so far that it lands on the moon. The crowds go wild for his phenomenal talent.
His proud family celebrates by carrying him on their shoulders around the town.
Every day for one hour, before everyone wakes up, he trains and celebrates.

One day, at breakfast, he tells his parents: "I want to become the world's best shot put athlete."
His mum chuckles. His dad whistles.
They all agree that he should start training as soon as possible.

Today is Saturday. The sun is shining very brightly on Tobias. He knows it's a good sign. Uri, his coach, gives him some tips on how to throw properly. His words don't reach Tobias. All he can focus on is the ball in his hand. It's much heavier than his red ball. He just can't wait to throw it.
"Ready?" Uri asks.
"Yes," replies Tobias.

He carefully places the ball on his neck. He silently summons the strengths of all the medieval shot putters who used to hurl cannonballs across the fields.
He spins, spins and spins.

Off he goes! Gripping the ball hard he finds himself lifting off the floor. He can see his mum and dad raised to their feet and waving their arms.
Up he goes, above the clouds, laughing and laughing more.

The wind gently carries him and he wonders
whether he will end up on the moon.
"This is the biggest throw of my life!"
he shouts.
"It certainly is," giggles the sun.
"You have reached 149 billion metres."
Tobias closes his eyes,
laughing more and more.

He opens his eyes and looks around.
He is back on the ground.
He hears his mum and dad cheering: "Hooray for Tobias!"
Uri approaches and bellows: "Well done Tobias! 1.49 metres!"

THE END

We are all... BACK AT SCHOOL! HOORAY!

Before our English lesson starts, let's play a game. Read carefully what each pupil says to find out which of these lovely autumnal clothes they love the most.

- YELLOW + BLUE = AWESOME!
- GLITTER IS COOL!
- I AM FOND OF FOXES
- BONES RULE!

All clothes are available from H&M Autumn 2012 collection currently in all stores around the UK & Ireland. Prices from £3.99. For your nearest stockist please telephone 0844 736 9000 or visit www.hm.com

WELCOME TO
ANORAK BROS

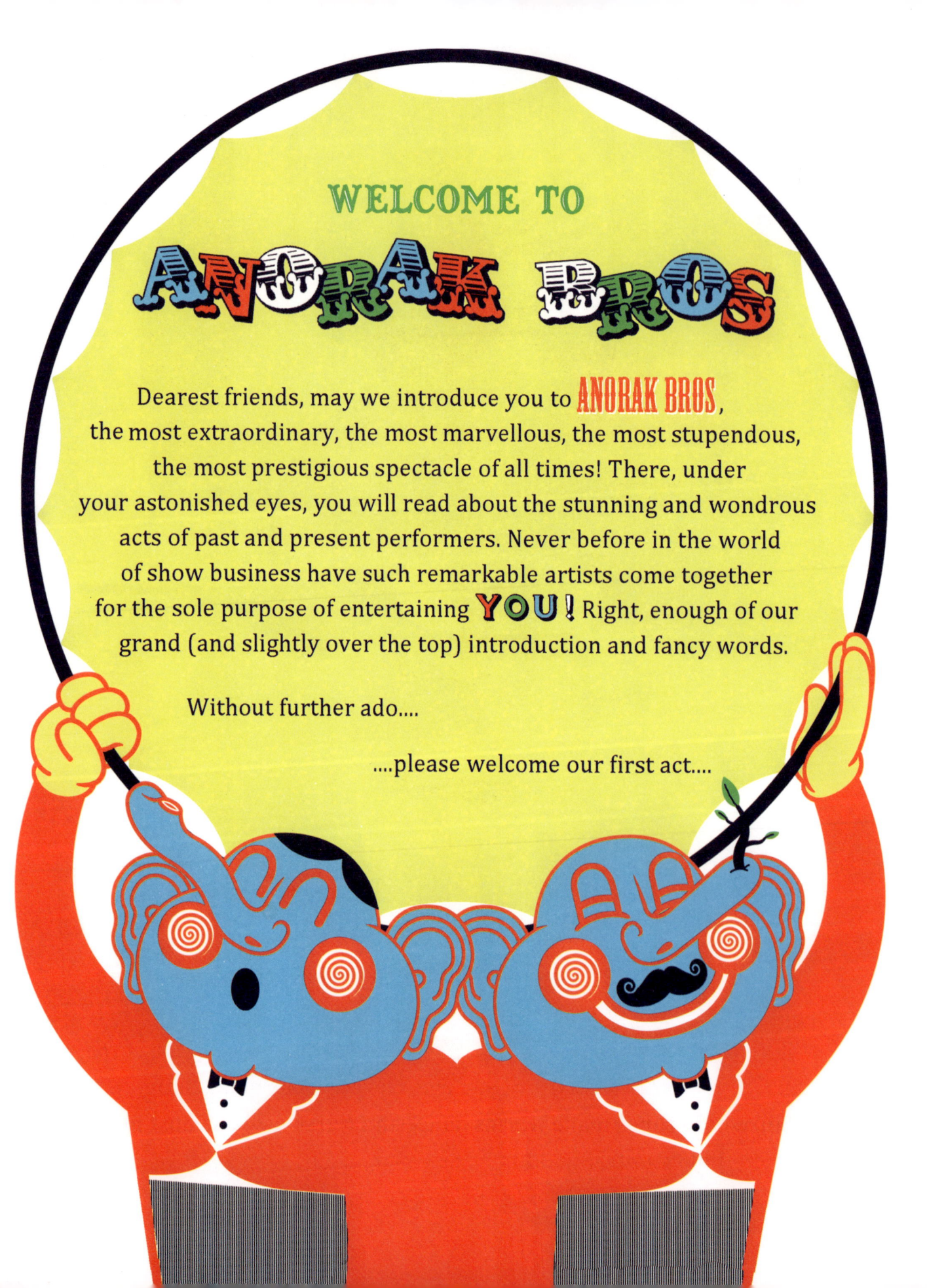

Dearest friends, may we introduce you to **ANORAK BROS**, the most extraordinary, the most marvellous, the most stupendous, the most prestigious spectacle of all times! There, under your astonished eyes, you will read about the stunning and wondrous acts of past and present performers. Never before in the world of show business have such remarkable artists come together for the sole purpose of entertaining **YOU**! Right, enough of our grand (and slightly over the top) introduction and fancy words.

Without further ado....

....please welcome our first act....

BEARDED LADYBIRD!

Dancing snails, worm charmers, bearded ladybirds, wasp tamers; the **INSECT CIRCUS** is a circus like no other. Established in 2006 and taking inspiration from 19th century music hall shows, it's simply one of the most inventive circuses we know of. So what can you expect to see at the Insect Circus? Dungo, the beetle who cleverly rolls on its dung; Tallulah, whose tunes make worms dance and Nursey, whose dust mites do incredible stunts. But don't be alarmed ....

....no insects are ever harmed in the shows!

ZANY CLOWN!

ZAZ ZAZ has been a clown since, well, early childhood! He tours up and down the country every day, leaving a trail of laughter behind him. Here's what we chatted about last time we caught up with him:

"I have always wanted to be a clown. Teachers used to tell me off all the time at school. "Stop clowning around," they'd say. But one day, when I was eight years old, I went to a clown festival. I joined in the fun and here I am, being a clown is now my job! I love my job as a clown. I get to have fun everywhere around the country performing circus tricks and making kids laugh. If you want to become a clown, I'd recommend you try a unicycle. It's fun and it's brilliant for fitness too. Kids always learn to ride quicker than adults, so don't be shy, give it a try!"

HUMAN CANNONBALL!

Being a daredevil is part of the ZACCHINI family's DNA, as they are the inventors of the human cannonball! Daddy Zacchini was a clever circus owner, who first tested the cannonball by hurling his son Hugo through the air! Thanks Dad! The first time his other son, Edmondo performed the same exploit in 1922, he broke a leg! Only a leg! Lucky, considering he had been thrown 20 feet up in the air! Nowadays, it's an American named David Smith who holds the record of the longest flight at 200ft! WHEEE!

INTREPID TRAPEZIST!

JACKIE is one talented lady. She is an aerialist. Which means she prefers to live up in the air rather than with her feet on the ground, like the rest of us. It's with our feet firmly on the ground that we caught up with her over a cup of tea.

"When I was a kid I loved trampoline and gymnastics. But it's after university that I decided to join the circus. Zippos Circus have a travelling school where you can train for six months. You train from 9am till 7pm every day. Once you are ready, you become a performer yourself. The toughest move I have had to learn is the 'neck hang'. It is really difficult to master as you need to find the right balance point. And it hurts a lot! It took me about six months to get it right! Just like anyone else, artists get scared sometimes. For me, swinging from a trapeze for the first time and throwing myself onto another was quite scary! We do two or three shows a day & help build the tent every day so that keeps me very fit. I would recommend to anyone who wants to join the circus to start with dance and gymastics classes at an early age. It teaches you coordination and grace, which you will need for any circus acts."

STRONGEST MAN IN THE WORLD!

If there is one man who deserves to be crowned the strongest man in the world, it certainly is **LOUIS CYR**; an extraordinary Canadian who lived during the early 20th century. The first time he entered a strongman competition, he simply managed to lift a horse off the ground. You know, easy, just like that! It is said that he could lift with his finger a whopping 500 pounds. That's not one, but two elephants' worth! With his finger! We are in awe.

EXTREME EQUILIBRIST!

KARL WALLENDA was simply a genius. At the tender age of six years old, he was already performing in theatre halls around Germany. Throughout his teens and twenties, he toured all over the world with a formidable show of high-wire walking. But it was in the mid 40s that he perfected an incredible balancing act, never seen before: the seven-person chair pyramid. It is difficult enough to imagine that with the chairs on the floor but imagine doing that on a wire AND 700 feet above ground AND with no nets! Since then, no one has been able to accomplish this exploit the way Karl and his family did.

We say BRAVO!

PIG LADY!

We love the fascinating legend of the Pig Lady! Dating as far back as the 17th century, it goes like this: a gentlewoman refused to hand over some money to a beggar who decided to put a curse on her. She and her children will be transformed into pigs!! This elusive Pig Lady was apparently seen in many places around England, Ireland & even Holland. During the 19th century, circuses were keen to capitalize on this enduring legend and the Pig Lady became a popular act. It was soon revealed that she was in fact a bear dressed in a delicate lady's outfit, with a shaved face and wearing a wig. Now that's grisly!

Do You Speak Circus?

Do You Rocker the Jib? Do You?

Let's put it in simple terms: to *rocker the jib* means to understand the language of the circus. *Parlari*, the language used by many circus owners & performers, has been around for centuries and amazingly, it is a mixture of Italian, French, Arabic, Yiddish & Irish. See if you can guess what we are saying here?

The **GAFFER** is a **DONAH** with the face of a **PUG!**
The **BOSS** is a **LADY** with the face of a **MONKEY!**

Are you ready to **SLANG** or you want to get some **KIP?**
Are you ready to **PERFORM** or you want to get some **SLEEP?**

NOW LET'S PLAY!

C	D	A	R	E	Z	E	P	A	R	T
A	L	P	R	E	D	N	O	S	E	R
N	L	O	P	O	C	F	D	E	D	E
D	I	P	W	G	L	M	A	I	O	D
Y	O	C	R	N	O	C	R	G	S	N
F	R	O	I	I	W	T	E	N	T	S
L	E	R	N	L	N	H	D	A	S	C
O	M	N	G	G	S	E	E	I	H	I
S	A	C	M	G	E	M	V	R	L	T
S	T	T	A	U	I	E	I	T	C	A
C	N	E	S	S	J	G	M	L	L	B
A	O	E	T	L	D	U	S	E	C	O
N	I	L	E	H	U	S	E	E	U	R
D	L	T	R	O	B	I	G	T	N	C
G	S	U	C	R	I	C	G	S	U	A

RED NOSE   DAREDEVILS   CANDY FLOSS
CLOWN   TRAPEZE   JUGGLING
LION TAMER   CIRCUS   UNICYCLIST
ACROBATICS   RING MASTER   STEEL TRIANGLE
POPCORN   BUDGIES   TENT
THEME MUSIC

MAKE STUFF

CIRCUS IN MY POCKET

TO MAKE THE CIRCUS PERFORMERS, YOU WILL NEED:
- ☐ Corks
- ☐ Polystyrene balls
- ☐ Toothpicks
- ☐ White tissue paper
- ☐ PVA glue

TO MAKE THE BOX, YOU WILL NEED:
- ☐ Mounting board
- ☐ Masking tape
- ☐ Wrapping paper

(tick off the boxes as you prepare)

First, let's make the box! Cut the mounting board into the shape of a matchbox drawer and sleeve. Stick together with masking tape. To make your box colourful, cover and line with different patterned wrapping paper.
We used craft paper on the outside so that when you pull out the drawer, it's a colour explosion!
The drawer when fully extended and turned upside down acts as a stage.

Now it's time to create the circus performers! Stick the toothpicks in the corks and add the polystyrene balls on top. Paint the heads with flesh coloured paint, and smudge red on the cheeks with the tip of your finger. When they are dry, use light pencil lines to draw the eyes, the mouth, the moustache and the clothes. Let your imagination run wild by creating different performers: a ballerina; a ring master; a weightlifter. Any characters you like!

You can give your performers hair by simply soaking strips of white tissue in PVA glue and sticking it to the heads. For example, for Nena, we used long strips of white tissue twisted and rolled to create a bun on the side.
If you would like to make the weightlifting barbells, simply use two polystyrene balls joined together by a toothpick and paint them black. The balloons are twisted bits of wire sandwiched between pieces of PVA coated tissue paper cut into balloon shapes.

Activity by Michelle McInerney.

NOW LET THE SHOW BEGIN!

MAKE IT TO THE TOP!

Guide Bob to the top of the mountain.

HELP ME!

Illustration by Nick Alston.

DRAW MY BODY BUDDY!

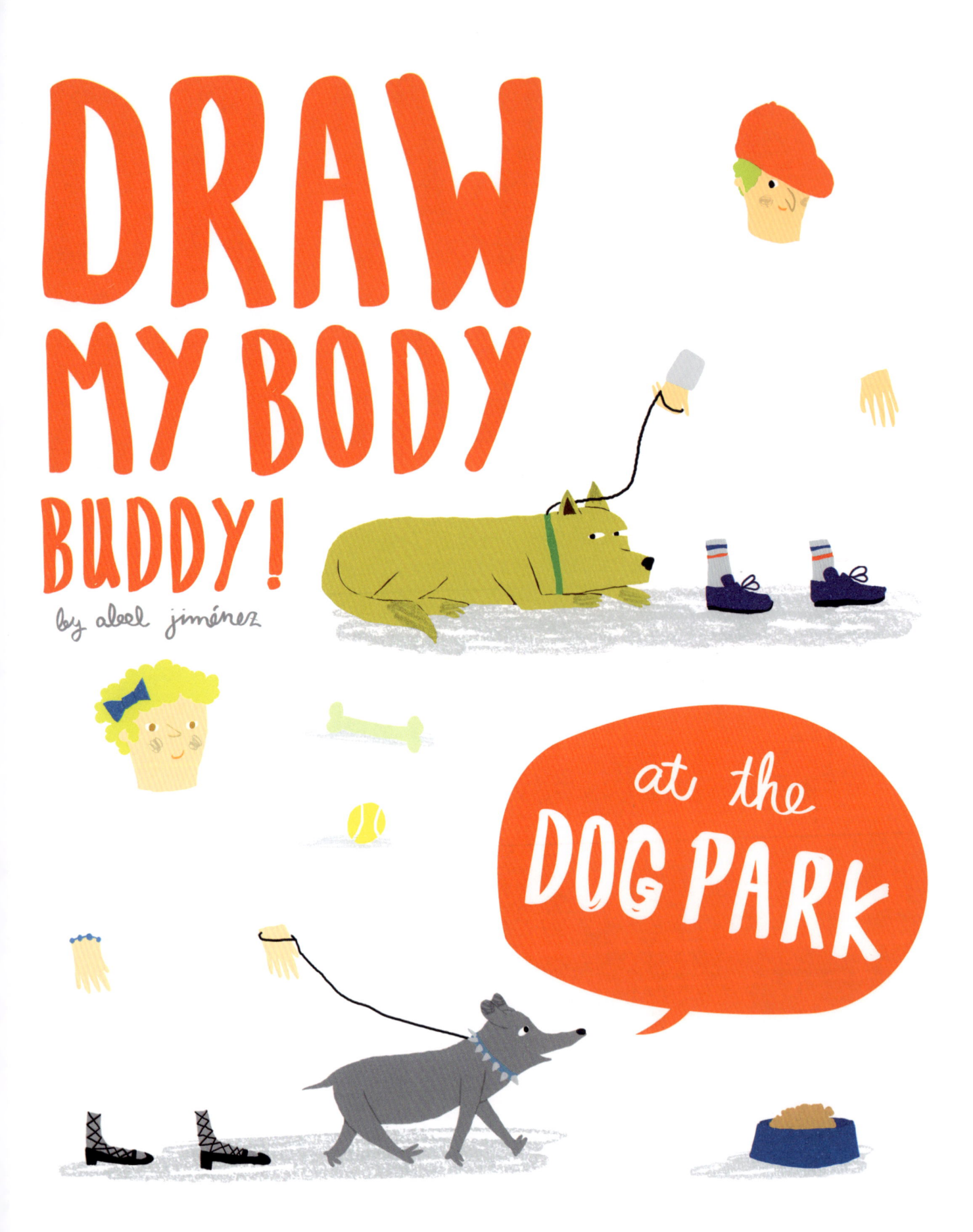

by abel jiménez

at the DOG PARK

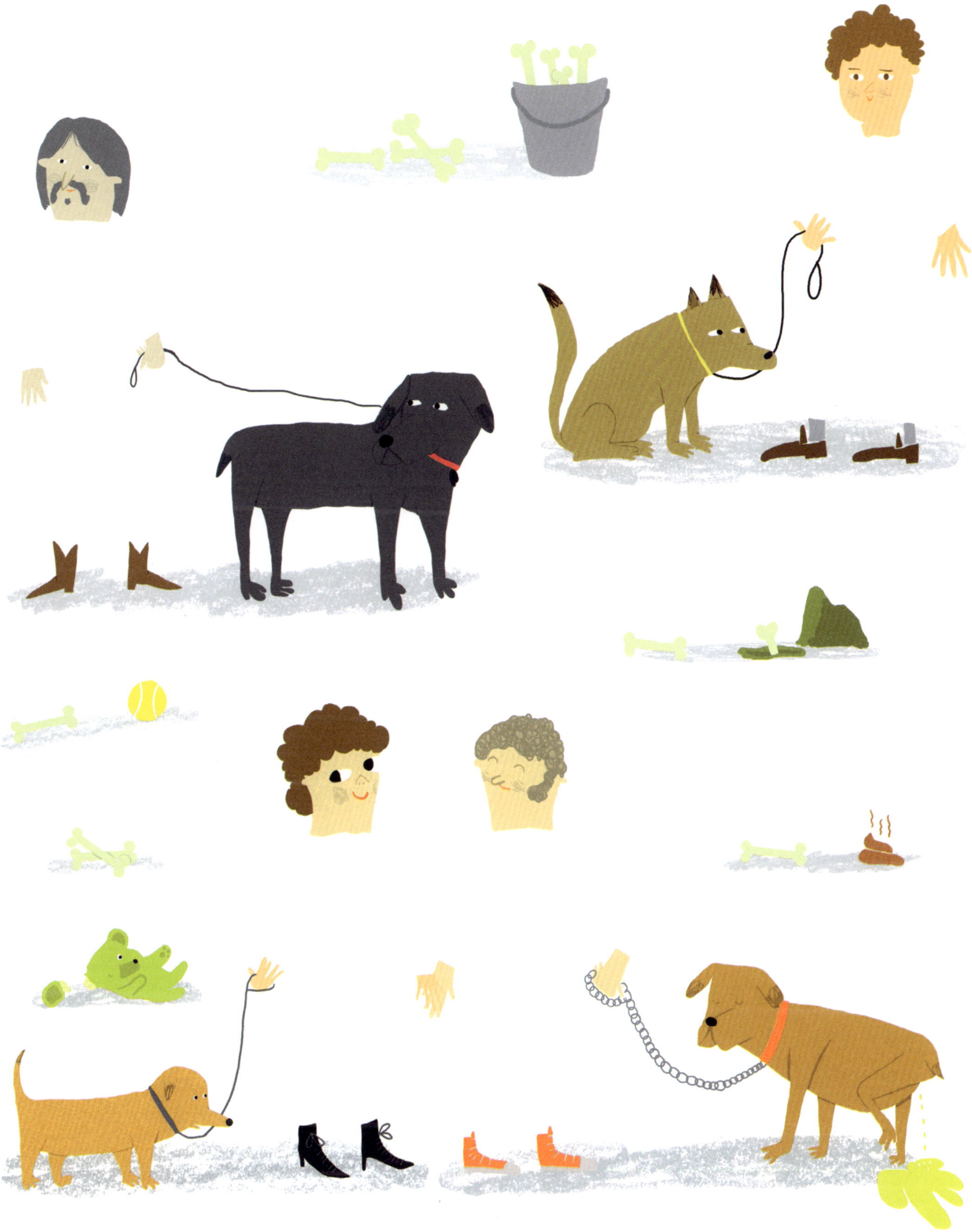

EAT STUFF

At Anorak, we love noodles. We could have noodles every day of the week, in fact we could have noodles for breakfast, noodles for tea and even noodles for dessert. This dish is one of our favourite Japanese dishes because it is not only tasty but it's also super easy to make. It's called YAKI SOBA which means 'Fried Noodles'.

We just call it **YUMMY SOBA**

CHOP CHOP STICKS STICKS

1.
Prepare Noodles as per packet instructions. Drain & Add a tablespoon of oil to stop them sticking and set aside till you need them.

You will need
- 1 Packet of Soba or rice noodles
- 350g Chicken thigh fillets, cut into strips (optional)
- 2 carrots, 1 onion
- 2 tablespoons toasted sesame seeds
- 2 spring onions, finely chopped
- A quarter head of Chinese cabbage finely cut
- 4 tablespoons of dark soya sauce
- 1 tablespoons of sugar, Sesame Oil
- canola oil for frying or normal vegetable oil if you can't find canola oil.

2.
TOAST sesame seeds lightly by dry roasting them in a shallow non stick frying pan on a medium heat. ONCE they become *golden* remove from the heat.

3.
CUT the onion in half and slice finely. Cut the carrots into thin strips (it's called a *Julienne* in proper Chef language!) and do the same with the Chinese cabbage and the spring onions.

4.
MIX the SOY, SUGAR and SESAME OIL in a small pan over a low heat. Stir well and pour over the chicken.

SOY, SUGAR, OIL

Heat your wok to smoking point. **5.**
Add oil *really really* carefully.
Add the chicken & stir until cooked. Remove & set aside in a bowl.

NOW FRY the onions till soft & ADD ALL the other vegetables EXCEPT Spring Onions (WAITING)

6. Stir & then ADD NOODLES. the CHICKEN and all its JUICES.

Add the spring onions and toss well.

7. REMOVE from the heat and sprinkle sesame all over it

TO SERVE, make little mountains

You can even add coriander leaves to make it prettier and tastier.

Make sure you make **LOTS** of noise as you slurp the noodles in! In Japan it is considered very polite to make noise to show you are enjoying your meal.

Recipe by Ruth Bruten. Illustration by Nanae Kawahara.

COLOUR IN!

Illustration by Mimi Leung.

SPOT THE DIFFERENCE!

Oops! There are ten differences between these two scenes. Can you spot them?

Illustration by Lara Elisa Carbone.

ANORAK HERO

In this issue of Anorak, it's not just one hero we worship but a whole bunch of them!
We first bumped into these chaps at a festival in our hometown in London
and instantly fell in love with this strange but brilliant family.
They are Delia and Uncle Burt, the vegetable nannies!
Here they introduce us to some of their favourite baby veggies.

"Hello Anorak readers! We are Delia and Uncle Burt and we grow and care for lots of baby vegetables on our allotment just outside Pontefract in Yorkshire, England. You might have heard of it, it's called Dribblesthwaite? Or maybe not as it only has a population of two. We like travelling to festivals but it's hard to catch any shows when you're babysitting all the time, so any help is welcome. Small people make the best carers and we are fortunate enough to be able to welcome lots of them into our allotment to lend a hand feeding, winding, cuddling, washing and reading stories to the babies. Usually we can only take a fraction of our allotment with us to festivals, as we don't have enough child seats in the van for everyone. Some of them get travel sick too, the cherry tomatoes are very unfortunate on that front."

"We feed all our babies liquid compost with a few added ingredients but the recipe is under wraps - patent pending."

"It's hard to pick a favourite. You can't, can you when they're your own? But we have some very special characters who we love dearly:

David the Marrow

David is a very sensitive marrow. He wants to be an actor when he grows up. Most marrows become trade vegetables, such as plumbers and plasterers, but he has caught the thespian bug. He has an audition for the Vegetable School of Speech and Drama next week, so he really is serious about becoming a professional. We have to remember he's still just a baby, though, and what he likes most of all is a cuddle and a bedtime story.

Barbara the Watermelon

Barbara is famous as she comes from a long line of "Downhill Racers". It involves melons from different parts of the world rolling down very steep hills, avoiding obstacles.
It can be quite treacherous: with rocks, brookes and the occasional sheep! Whilst rolling Barbara can reach a full speed of 30 mph! She is a bit of a daredevil as you may have guessed!

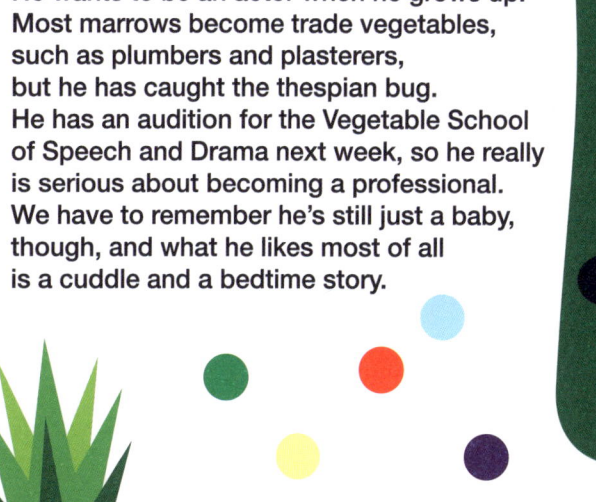

Cindy the Pineapple

Cindy is just visiting from the Caribbean. She's been with us for three weeks now and is a very extrovert character. She wants to be a hairdresser when she grows up and is always trying out her hairdressing skills on the other babies.
She does have nits at the moment though.

Hercules the Potato

Ah Hercules! We're very proud of him at the moment as he's just got his black belt in Jiu-Jitsu. He is our bouncer on the allotment. He has proved himself on many occasions; fighting off stray slugs and snails that venture in looking to cause trouble. Hercules's heroic antics have also led to him sweeping Jessica, another Potato, off her feet. She doesn't have feet, but you know what we mean. She swooned! They often sit by the gate and watch the sunset together. How sweet!"

For more info on The Vegetable Nannies, check out their website www.plungeboom.com

GOOD TIMES

Illustration by Dan Woodger.

MAKE THIS PARTY EVEN MORE FUN BY ADDING SOME COLOUR!

ANORAK MAGAZINE IS THE HAPPY MAG FOR KIDS

Founding Editor: Cathy Olmedillas
Cover & main feature: Rob Flowers
Chief Subber: Stephanie Lynn
Chief Designer: Evgenia Barinova
Writers: Nathan & Emma Cooper, Ruth Bruten aka Gourmet Girlfriend, Michelle McInerney and Dexter Robinson (8 years old).
Illustrators, drawers and doodlers: Dan Woodger, Orson Coupland, Nanae Wakahara, Abel Jimenez, Mimi Leung, Simon Wild, Lara Elisa Carbone, James Clapham and Nick Alston.

A warm thank you to Sarah & Mark from the Insect Circus Museum www.insectcircus.co.uk, Jackie at Zippos Circus www.zipposcircus.co.uk and Zaz the clown www.zazismypal.com

Subscribe to Anorak Magazine

Why? Because your Mum & Dad will save money! And because you get Anorak delivered straight to your bedroom door. It makes so much sense!! To subscribe, please visit our site anorakmagazine.com.

Anorak is published five times a year by OKSAR LTD. Reproduction of editorial is strictly prohibited without prior permission.
Copyright OKSAR LTD. 2012. All rights reserved.
8 Soda Studios, 268 Kingsland Road, London E8 4DG.
Anorak ™ is a registered trademark by OKSAR LTD.
Trademark number 2548950.
Anorak is printed on FSC® certified paper.

Please visit our happy website for list of stockists, subscriptions and other fun!
www.anorakmagazine.com

Anorak North America

Anorak North America is co-published with Gibbs Smith,
PO Box 667 Layton, Utah 84041.
For info and subscriptions, please visit
www.anorakmagazine.com/northamerica

Anorak TV

Did you know? Anorak is not just a paper magazine, it's also a TV programme! It contains interviews with artists, stories, games and kids who tell jokes and draw. To see a preview of Anorak TV, go to our YouTube channel (youtube.com/anorakmagazine) and to download the full 20-minute episode, go to the Apple store and search for HAPPY TV!